max science primary

DISCOVERING THROUGH ENQUIRY

Workbook 6

LAWRIE RYAN

SERIES EDITOR: BOB KIBBLE

macmillan education

INTERNATIONAL CURRICULUM

Macmillan Education
4 Crinan Street
London N1 9XW
A division of Springer Nature Limited

Companies and representatives throughout the world

Workbook ISBN 978-1-380-02172-4

First published 2019

Original design by EMC Design Ltd and Macmillan Education
Page make-up by Ink Design
Illustrated by Nick L'Ange, Alistair Ackermann, Chris Venter, Sean Strydom, Marna Hattingh
Nick L'Ange pp 1, 2, 3, 10, 18, 22, 40, 70, 79, 90, 96; Alistair Ackermann pp 8, 9, 17, 30, 31, 34, 44, 46, 48, 50; Chris Venter pp 26, 27, 28, 93; Sean Strydom pp 55, 56, 57, 60, 62, 63, 64; Marna Hattingh pp 58, 68, 71, 95, 96, 99
Cover design by Sparks Publishing Services Ltd and Macmillan Education
Cover illustration by Star Publishing Pte Ltd and Jorge Santillan c/o Beehive Illustration Agency
Picture research by Susannah Jayes

The author and publishers would like to thank the following for permission to reproduce their photographs:
Getty Images/Andrew Baranowski p26(tl), Getty Images/Benjamins, Sven p26(tr);
Lawrie Ryan p41(A, B , C, D).

Printed and bound in the UK by Bell and Bain Ltd, Glasgow
2023 2022 2021 2020 2019
10 9 8 7 6 5 4 3 2 1

Contents

Introducing the *Max Science primary* Workbook

The ***Max Science primary* Workbooks** accompany the **Student Book** for class and home use. All the numbered activities and extension activities found in the Student Book are expanded with clear answer spaces and support. Instructions carefully show if activities are to be done independently, in pairs or in groups.

Practising my science language

Supported activities focus on improving scientific literacy to make the learning of science through the medium of English more accessible.

Extending understanding

Extension questions encourage learners to go a bit further to improve the depth of understanding.

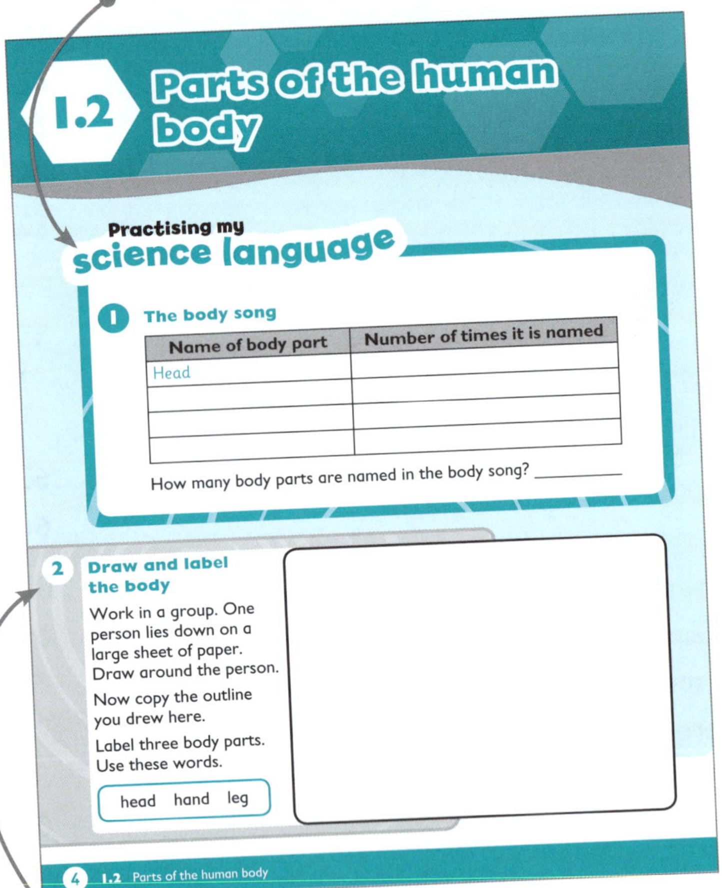

1.2 Parts of the human body

Practising my science language

1 The body song

Name of body part	Number of times it is named
Head	

How many body parts are named in the body song? ______

2 Draw and label the body

Work in a group. One person lies down on a large sheet of paper. Draw around the person.

Now copy the outline you drew here.

Label three body parts. Use these words.

head hand leg

4 1.2 Parts of the human body

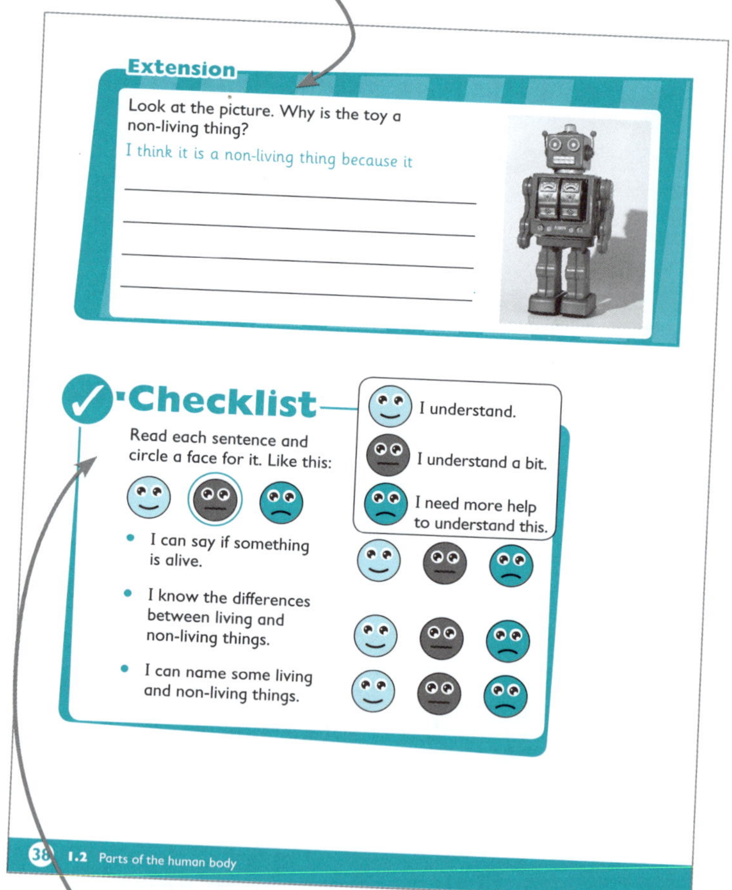

Extension

Look at the picture. Why is the toy a non-living thing?

I think it is a non-living thing because it

Checklist

Read each sentence and circle a face for it. Like this:

I understand.

I understand a bit.

I need more help to understand this.

- I can say if something is alive.
- I know the differences between living and non-living things.
- I can name some living and non-living things.

38 1.2 Parts of the human body

Exploring science further

Numbered activities from the Student Book are expanded with example answers for guidance. Learners can record their scientific progress, insights and results.

Assessing progress

End-of-topic checklists provide opportunities for recording what learners have learnt so far.

1 Human organs and systems

1 All about my body

a. Look at the example mind map started below. Draw one like it on paper to map out what you know about the human body.

Use the words in the box.

- Label the links between the words.
- Then add some of your own words.

food and water	skeleton	organs	senses

b. Swap mind maps with a partner. Add any new ideas from your partner to your mind map.

c. What is the word used to describe food and drink taken into the body?

____

Add this word to your mind map.

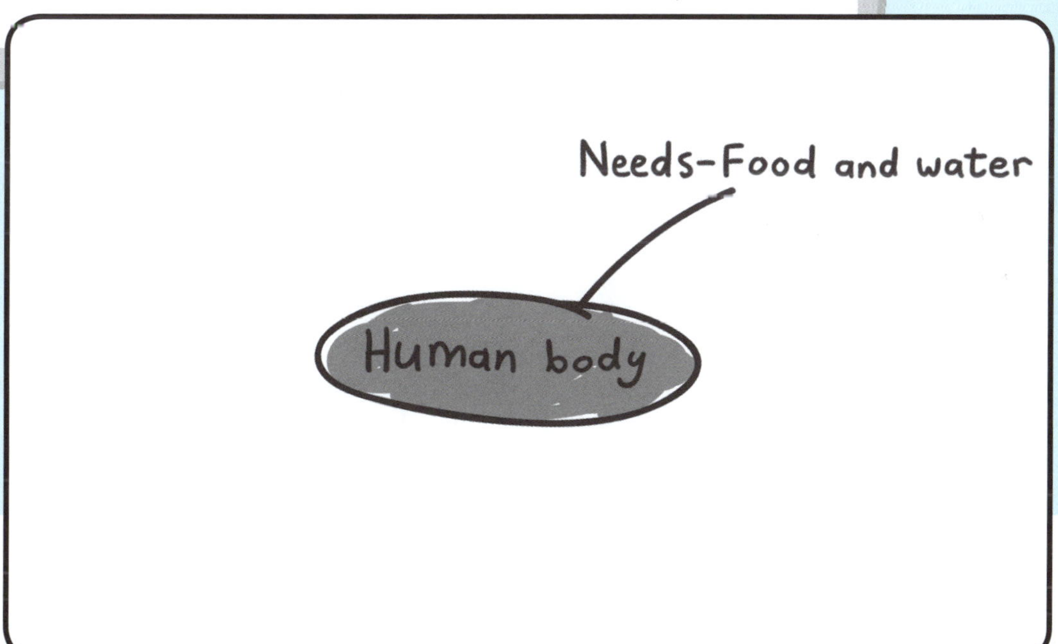

2 Where are our organs?

Draw and label the correct positions and shapes of the following organs on the outline of the human body:

heart   lungs   kidneys   liver   stomach   brain

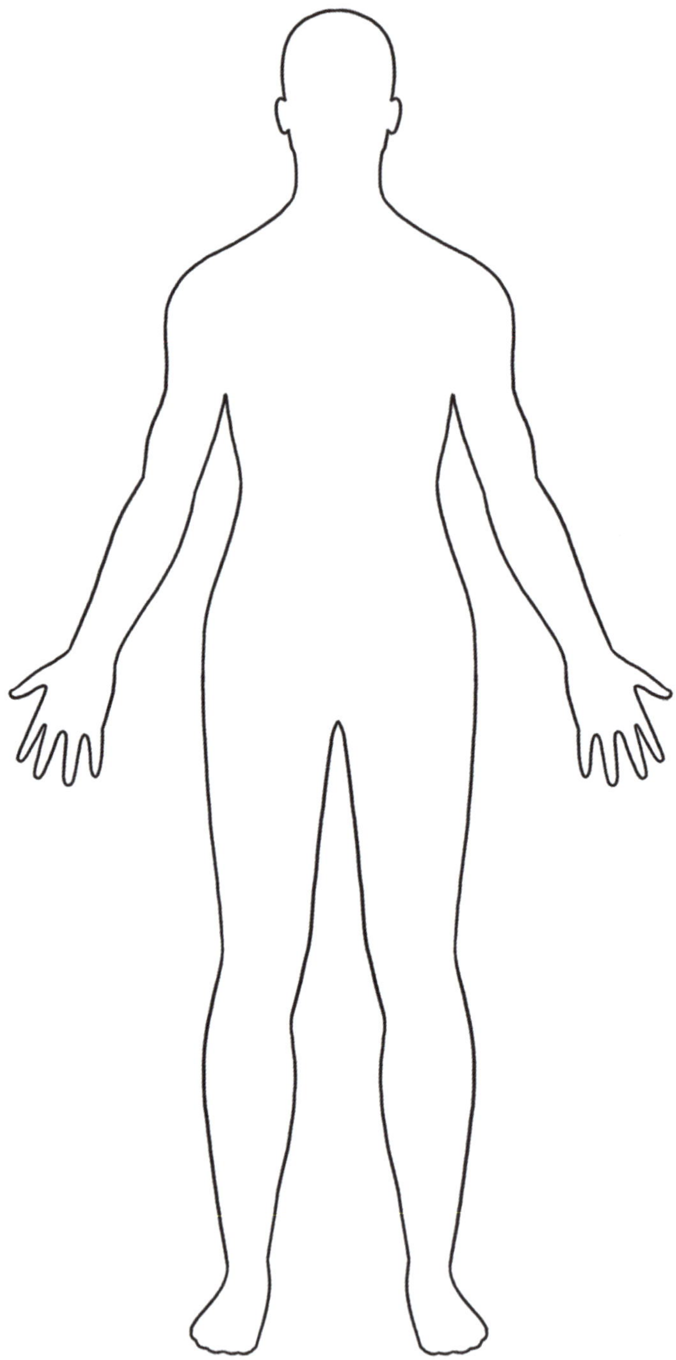

1.1 Why do we need organs?

Practising my science language

1 Life processes

a. Talk to your partner about nutrition, movement, growth and reproduction. Fill in the missing words to show what each of the processes mean.

Choose the correct word from this list:

size food offspring position

Nutrition: In this process a living thing takes in _____________ to get things it needs to stay alive.

Movement: In this process a living thing changes its _____________.

Growth: In this process a living thing changes its _____________ as it gets bigger.

Reproduction: In this process living things produce new _____________.

b. Can you think of three other processes that living things must do?

Cover the list of hints on the next page before you start. If your group gets stuck, uncover them one by one.

Process 1 ____

Process 2 ____

Process 3 ____

Hint

- **Process 1:** You use these to detect what is happening to you. (Even plants use these, for example, when they grow towards a source of light.) They can help living things avoid danger.
- **Process 2:** What happens to the materials left after a living thing has taken what it needs from its food and water?
- **Process 3:** This process enables living things to use food as a fuel. What do we get from all fuels?

2 Have I improved?

a. With your Student Book closed, repeat Activity 2 *Where are our organs?* from page 2. Draw and label the shape and position of the major organs of the human body.

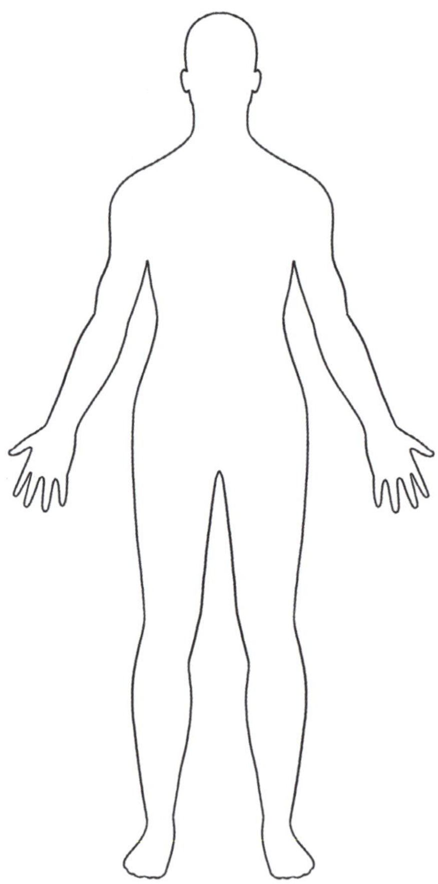

b. Now check your drawing against the diagram on page 5 in the Student Book.

Have you done better than last time? **Yes** **No**

Extension

A Stage 4 class is doing a project about staying healthy. They need a good, clear poster to help them learn about the organs in their bodies.

Work with a partner to design and create a poster for the Stage 4 class that shows the major organs of the human body and **explains** why we need each of them.

Checklist

Read each sentence and circle a face for it. Like this:

I understand.

I understand a bit.

I need more help to understand this.

- I can identify the position of major organs in the body.
- I can explain why the major organs are essential.

1.2 Body systems and organs

1 The first stage in digestion

What happens to the taste when you chew a small piece of bread without swallowing it?

____

How does the "feel" of the bread change inside your mouth?

____

What do you think is happening to the bread in your mouth?

____

Practising my science language

2 Compare the air we breathe in with the air we breathe out

Work with a partner. Look at the table below and answer the questions.

Gas	Air we breathe in (%)	Air we breathe out (%)
Oxygen	21	16
Carbon dioxide	0.04	4

Circle the correct options in bold:

a. The amount of oxygen gas in the air we breathe in is **lower / higher** than in the air we breathe out.

b. The amount of carbon dioxide gas in the air we breathe in is much **lower / higher** than in the air we breathe out.

3 What is in your breath?

a. What do you notice when you breathe out onto the back of your hand?

____

____

b. Work with a partner. What do you observe on the surface of a small mirror when you wave it through the air?

____

____

Now breathe out onto the surface of the mirror. What do you observe? Think back to your work on the changing states of water.

____

____

c. Explain your **observations**. Circle the correct options in bold:

The air we breathe out is **warmer than / colder than / the same as** the air we breathe in.

The air we breathe out contains **less / more / the same amount of** water vapour as the air we breathe in.

4 Other organs involved in excretion

Work in a small group.

a. **Name** a waste material that is passed from the body to the lungs and breathed out.

____

b. What waste materials are passed out through your skin?

____

____

5 Checking progress so far!

a. Which numbered statements, **1** to **6**, are true and which are false? Write each number in the correct column below.

True statements	False statements

b. Correct Basma's statements that are false. Write your corrected statements below.

____

____

____

Extension

When we exercise, our heart beats faster and we breathe more quickly.

Why do you think both of these things happen together?

____

____

____

6 Check your reaction time

Work with a partner to check each other's reaction time.

You can use an app or visit a website to do your tests. Put "reaction time tester" into a search engine.

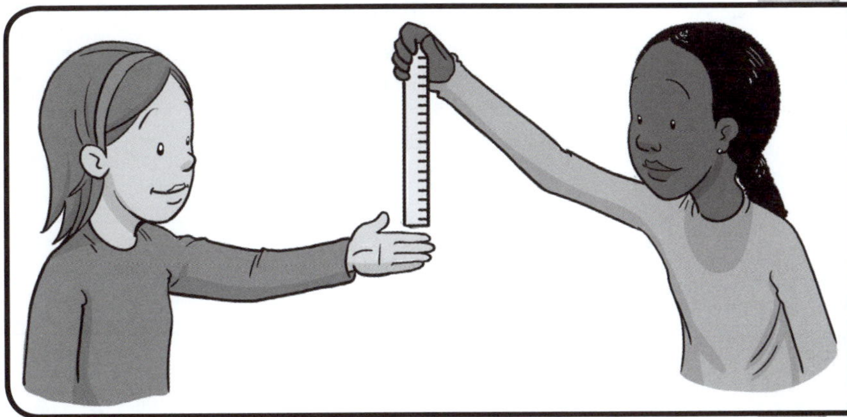

If you do not have access to the internet, try this simple alternative activity, where you try to catch a ruler as quickly as you can after your partner drops it.

a. If you are right-handed, is your left hand as fast to react as your right hand (or vice-versa if you are left-handed)? **Yes** **No**

b. Design a fair test to investigate this question.

___

___

___

c. How will you ensure your tests are reliable? Think about these things:

- Will the results apply to one person or most people?
- How many times did you repeat the test?
- Did you get faster as you did more tests?

___

___

___

___

d. Make a prediction and record your observations.

___

___

___

___

e. Write your conclusion. Who had the faster reactions? ___

7 Summary time

Complete the summary table of the organ systems and their major organs to check your understanding.

Organ system	Major organs in the system
Digestive system	
Respiratory system	
Excretory system	
Circulatory system	
Nervous system	

Extension

a. Find out what hormones are and where they are made in your body.

____

____

____

____

____

b. Draw a diagram of the body system that transports hormones around your body.

c. Give two examples of the changes hormones cause in the human body.

1 ______________________________

2 ______________________________

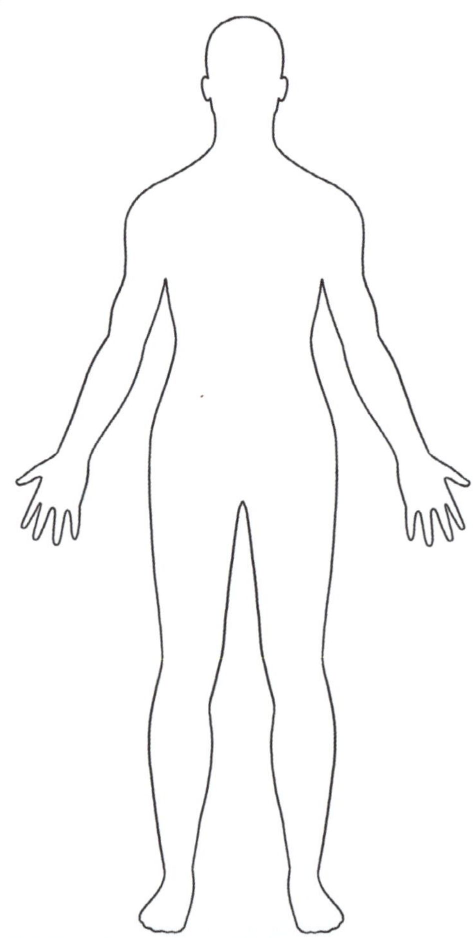

✓ Checklist

Read each sentence and circle a face for it. Like this:

- I understand.
- I understand a bit.
- I need more help to understand this.

- I can describe the functions of the major organs of the body (stomach/intestines, lungs, kidneys, heart, brain).
- I can name the body system each major organ belongs to.

1.3 When organs go wrong

1 What we already know about illnesses

Draw a table to summarise any illnesses or conditions that can affect each organ listed below, and their symptoms.

stomach lungs kidneys heart brain

Practising my

science language

2 Research organ malfunction

Choose one organ from the box below and find out about:

- an illness or condition that affects your chosen organ
- the symptoms of the illness or condition
- how the illness or condition can be treated or if it can be cured.

stomach	lungs	kidneys	heart	brain

Which organ have you chosen to research?

____

Name an illness or condition that affects this organ.

____

Describe the symptoms:

____

____

____

Describe how the illness or condition can be treated. Can it be cured?

____

____

____

____

Extension

Write a list of six body parts that can be transplanted from one person to another.

1 ______________________________

2 ______________________________

3 ______________________________

4 ______________________________

5 ______________________________

6 ______________________________

Checklist

Read each sentence and circle a face for it. Like this:

I understand.

I understand a bit.

I need more help to understand this.

- I can describe why some organs may stop working properly.
- I can describe what, if anything, can be done to treat the problems.
- I can carry out scientific research.
- I can report my findings clearly.

Glossary

In your own language, write down what these words mean:

body

____

____

brain

____

____

breathing

____

____

circulation

____

____

control

____

____

cure

____

____

digestion

____

____

disease

____

____

excretion

____

____

function

____

____

Glossary

heart

intestines

kidneys

liver

lungs

major organs

organ

stomach

symptom

system

2 Reversible and irreversible changes

1 What happens when an ice lolly changes?

Benita is thinking about what happens to the materials in an ice lolly when it changes in some way:

a. Is an ice lolly one material or is it a mixture of materials? Circle the correct answer in bold below.

An ice lolly is a **pure material / a mixture of materials**.

b. In groups, think about whether the materials in the ice lolly change or whether they are the same materials after the change.

- Which of Benita's ideas do you agree with? ____________________
- Which of Benita's ideas do you disagree with? ____________________

c. Write down any of your own ideas.

____

____

2.1 Investigating reversible and irreversible changes

1 Changes in the kitchen

a. Think about the changes you can see when meals are prepared:

A

Heating butter in a pan

B

Cooking an egg in a pan

C

Baking a cake

D

Making a poppadum or fritter

E

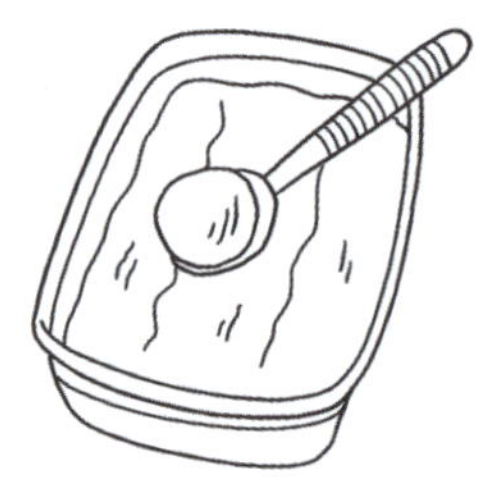

Making ice-cream in a freezer

b. Can you get the food back to what it was before you started, or is that impossible? Discuss the changes with a partner, then answer "Yes" or "No" in the table below. One has been done for you.

Can the food change back to what it was before?	Yes / No
A Heating butter in a pan	
B Cooking an egg in a pan	
C Baking a cake	No
D Making a poppadum or fritter	
E Making ice-cream in a freezer	

Practising my

science language

2 Up or down?

Work with a partner.

a. Decide which of the following reversible changes happen when the temperature increases and which happen when the temperature decreases.

- melting
- freezing
- boiling
- condensing

Record your answers in the table below. One has been done for you.

When temperature increases	When temperature decreases
	freezing

b. Think about water. Are the particles that make up water any different in ice, liquid water and steam? Circle the correct answer. **Yes** **No**

c. What change happens to the particles in water when the temperature changes? Complete the sentences:

The particles of water get f________ apart or c________ together.

The particles of water move more s________ or more q________.

d. Is a new material formed when a material changes state? Circle the correct answer. **Yes** **No**

3 Hot chocolate

a. Describe what you see when a piece of chocolate is heated.

____

____

b. Has the chocolate changed into a different material? Circle the correct answer. **Yes** **No**

4 Examples of reversible changes

Think about the examples of reversible changes in A to D, below. Then with a partner, answer the questions. Use these words to help you.

cool	hot	melting	freezing	water	water vapour	condenses

A Laying a new road with hot, sticky tarmac

Why can cars not drive on a new tarmac road for a couple of days?

____

____

B Defrosting (not cooking) a frozen meal

Which material is changing state when we defrost a frozen meal?

____

Name the change of state taking place. ______________

If you turn the microwave oven on too high, what will you see coming out of the oven when you open its door? Explain why.

____

____

What will happen to this material when it meets a cold surface?

____

C Using chocolate to ice a cake

Describe the changes of state when you ice a cake using a bar of chocolate to start with.

____

____

D Making gold rings

The jeweller starts with solid gold to make rings.

What do icing the cake with chocolate and making gold rings have in common?

Both chocolate and gold ______________________________.

How are they different?

They are different because ______________________________.

5 Observing an irreversible change

Record your observations when you add bicarbonate of soda to vinegar in a yoghurt pot. Use these words to help you:

fizzing bubbling foam heat

What do you see happen?

I can see ______________________________

______________________________.

What can you hear?

I can hear ______________________________

______________________________.

Hold the outside of the yoghurt pot near the bottom. What can you feel?

I can feel ______________________________

______________________________.

6 Strike a light!

Record your observations as your teacher strikes a match and lets it burn.

How did your teacher make the match start burning?

____

Why is this an irreversible change?

I classify this as an irreversible change because ______________________________

____

______________________________.

7 Does burning use up gas from the air?

Watch your teacher carry out a demonstration by covering a tea-light candle with a beaker.

a. Record all your observations once the beaker covers the tea-light.

____

____

b. Complete the diagram to show what happened.

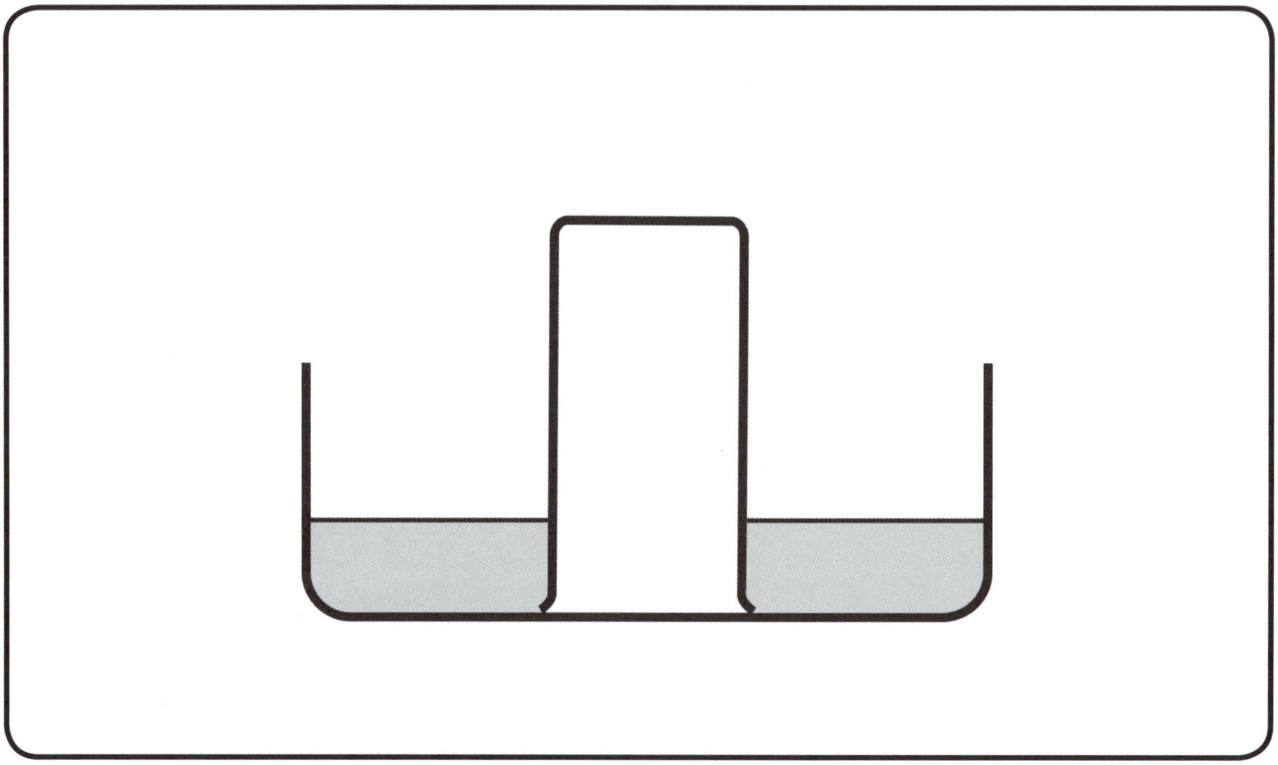

c. Explain why the tea-light flame went out. This is the conclusion from the experiment.

The tea-light flame went out because ____

____

____.

Extension

Plan an investigation to find out if different types of paper burn for different lengths of time. Include these points:

a. How will you make it a fair test? Which variables (factors) will you keep the same?

b. What equipment will you need to carry out a safe test?

c. How can you check how reliable your results are?

d. What type of graph will you use to display the results?

____

____

____

____

____

____

____

____

Extension

a. Water is used to put out fires. What else helps to put out fires?

____

____

b. Write some rules to avoid accidental fires starting in the home.

____

____

____

c. Use your findings to create a poster to display to the rest of the class.

8 Apply your knowledge

a. Observe a candle burning.

b. Describe and explain the reversible and irreversible changes taking place.

When a candle burns the reversible change is ______________________________

____

____.

When a candle burns the irreversible change is ____________________________

____

____.

Checklist

Read each sentence and circle a face for it. Like this:

I understand.

I understand a bit.

I need more help to understand this.

- I know how to distinguish between reversible and irreversible changes.
- I can classify everyday changes as reversible or irreversible.
- I know about burning as an example of an irreversible change.

2.2 Making and separating mixtures

Practising my science language

1 Separating mixtures of solids

a. With a partner, mix some dry rice grains and dried peas together in an empty yoghurt pot.

- Have the rice or peas turned into a new material? Circle the correct answer.

  Yes **No**

- What type of change is this? Circle the correct answer.

  Reversible / Irreversible

- Explain how you can separate the rice from the peas. Complete the sentence:

  The rice grains are smaller than the peas so we can ______________________
  ____
  ____
  ____

b. Now mix rice grains with flour, stirring them up. Try to separate the flour from the rice.

- Explain why it is easy to get pure flour but not so easy to get pure rice. Fill in the two missing words:

  The rice grains have some ______________ stuck to their surface but most of the flour passes through the ______________.

- Think of a way to remove any flour stuck to the rice.

  To remove the flour, I think that we could ______________________
  ____
  ____

2 Applications of sieving

A tea-strainer in action

Boiled vegetables are "strained" before they are served.

a. Explain what is happening in the two photos above.

Tea strainer:

____

____

Straining vegetables:

____

____

b. In a water treatment plant, water from a river passes through a large metal grid before entering the plant.

What is the purpose of the metal grid?

The purpose of the metal grid is

____

____

____

_______________________________.

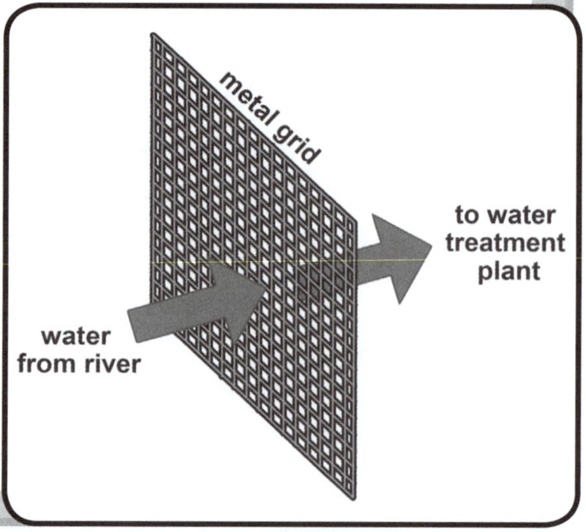

3 Remember filtration!

Here are the pieces of **equipment** and materials that you need to filter a mixture of sand, salt and water:

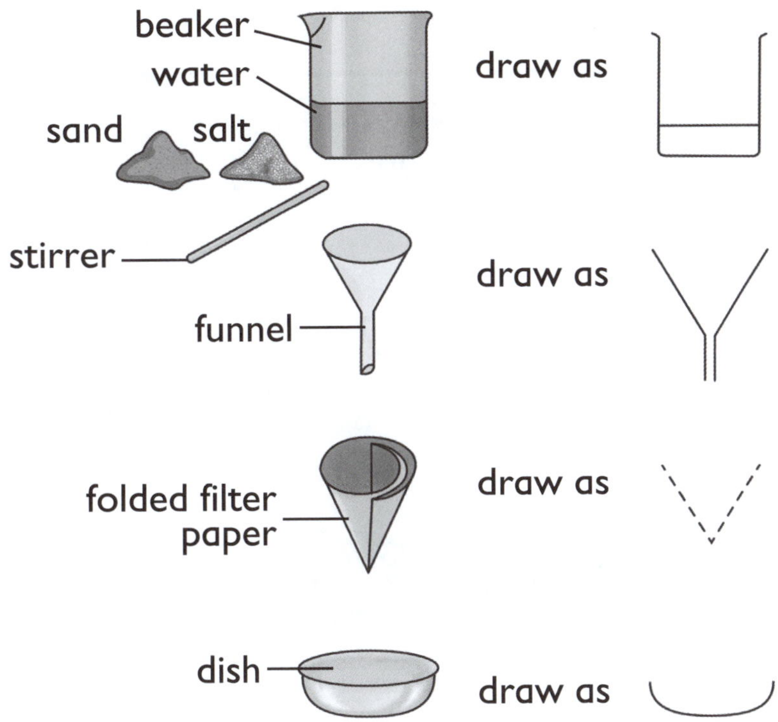

Work in a pair. Your task is to find a way to separate the sand from the salt solution.

a. Draw a science diagram of the filtration **apparatus** in action. Use the equipment drawn on the right-hand side of the diagram above.

b. Describe how you can separate the salt from the colourless solution collected in the dish.

I can separate the salt from the solution by ____________________

____

____

____________________.

4 Modelling the filtration used in a water treatment plant

You can model the water treatment plant's filtration process in a yoghurt pot.

a. Set up the apparatus shown below:

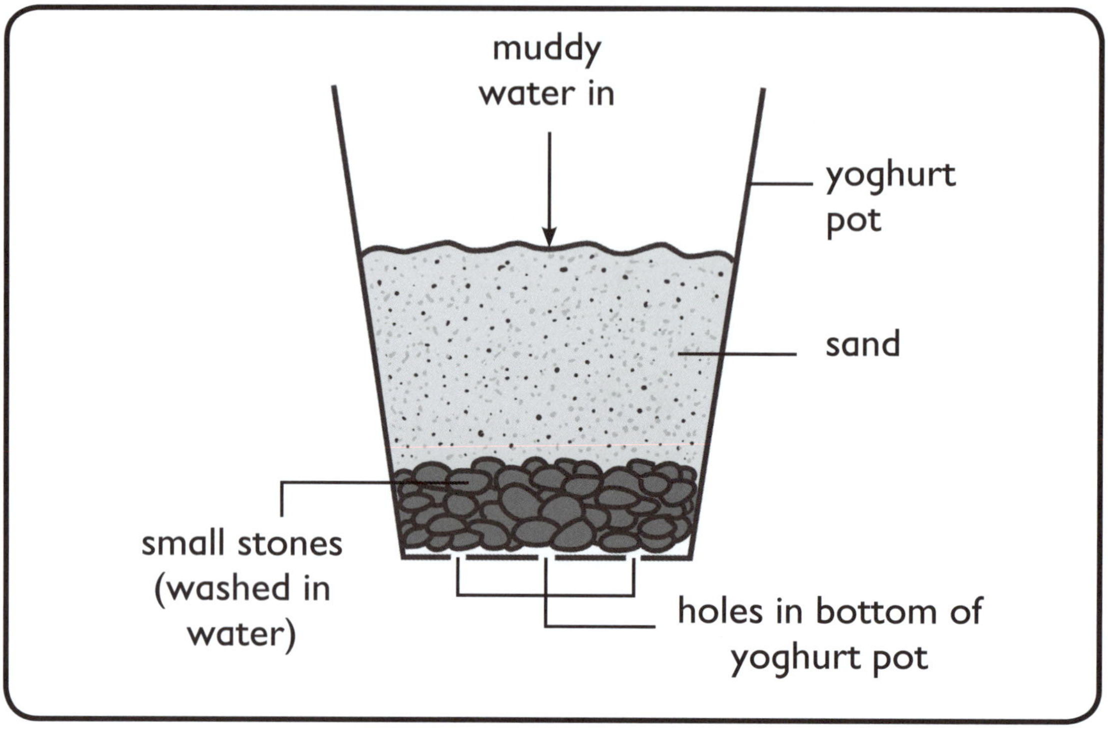

b. Compare the muddy water with the water filtered through the sand.

____

____

____

____

c. What can you do to make the water even clearer?

____

____

____

____

____

Extension

Think about filtering the water in a water treatment plant.

How can you remove as many insoluble solids as possible using sand filtration?

- Will two filter tanks help?
- What about the thickness of the layer of sand and the length of time the water takes to get through the sand?

Write down your ideas.

____

____

____

____

Checklist

Read each sentence and circle a face for it. Like this:

I understand.

I understand a bit.

I need more help to understand this.

- I can observe and record what happens when we mix solids.
- I know how to separate mixtures of solids.
- I know when to use filtration to separate mixtures.

2.3 Dissolving

1 Ideas about dissolving

In the table below, write down which numbers (1 to 4) you:

- agree with
- do not agree with
- are not sure about.

I agree with:	I do not agree with:	I am not sure about:

2 Growing sugar crystals

Describe and draw your results from this experiment.

3 Does it dissolve?

a. With a partner, plan a test to see which of the materials provided for you dissolve in water and which are insoluble. Include a torch to test any materials that are tricky to judge.

____

____

____

____

b. Carry out your test and record your results in a table.

c. Which materials were difficult to classify as soluble or insoluble?

____

Extension

Watch your teacher add white plaster of Paris powder slowly to water and stir.

Record and explain the changes you observe after 45 minutes and after three days.

Observations after 45 minutes	Observations after 3 days

2.4 More about dissolving

1 Modelling the process of dissolving

a. In pairs, plan how you can use your classmates to create a human model to show what happens as a solid **dissolves** in **water**. Some people can be water particles and others can be particles of a soluble solid, such as sugar.

Answer the following questions to help you:

- How many people will you need?

  ____

- How will they be arranged in the solid?

  ____

- How will they be arranged in water (a liquid)?

  ____

- What is the difference between the movement of the tiny particles in a solid and in water?

  ____

- What do you think happens to the particles of solid as they dissolve into the water?

  ____

- How are the solid and water particles arranged in the solution? Will they be moving around?

  ____

b. **Describe** what happens to the particles of a solid when it dissolves in water.

____

____

____

2 Pure or mixture?

Your teacher will give you two liquids. One is a pure material and one is a solution. The solution is a **mixture** of water and a **soluble** solid.

Plan a simple investigation below to find out which liquid is pure and which is a solution.

____

____

____

____

3 Choosing equipment

You will be given these different types of sugar to investigate:

- sugar cubes
- icing sugar
- granulated sugar
- brown sugar.

Your task is to find out which type of sugar dissolves most quickly.

a. What **equipment** will you need to do this investigation? Work in groups and think about what you will need to:

- dissolve sugar
- measure how quickly the sugar dissolves.

____

____

____

b. Will you need to measure anything else to make sure it is a fair test?

____

Practising my

science language

4 Which type of sugar dissolves most quickly?

a. Predict the order in which the different sugars in Activity 3 will dissolve, with the fastest first. Use the words in the box to help you.

sugar cubes	icing sugar	granulated sugar	brown sugar

1 ____________ 2 ____________

3 ____________ 4 ____________

Explain your order.

I think that ____________ will dissolve the fastest because

____________________________________.

I think that ____________ will dissolve the slowest because

____________________________________.

b. Now carry out your investigation, making your tests as fair as possible.

- Which variables (factors) will you need to keep the same to carry out a fair test?

  ____

  ____

  ____

- Is it easy to see exactly when all the sugar has dissolved?

  ____

- Are your timings very accurate?

  ____

- What is the best way to make them more reliable?

  ____

  ____

continues on following page ...

... continued from previous page

c. Record your results in the table below. Include all repeat readings and the "average (mean) time to dissolve" for each type of sugar.

Type of sugar	Time for sugar to dissolve in seconds			
	1st try	2nd try	3rd try	Average

d. Draw a bar chart on a piece of graph paper to show your results. Make sure you draw a separate bar for each type of sugar tested. Use your average (mean) times for the height of each bar. You can stick your graph into your Workbook.

e. Was your prediction correct? Circle your answer. **Yes** **No**
Explain how the evidence you collected shows this.

____

____

5 How does temperature affect how quickly sugar dissolves?

a. Predicting

- Predict the pattern you expect to find.

  The higher the temperature ____________________________

  ____.

b. Carrying out and recording

- Fill in the headings and record your results in the table below. Your teacher will help you work out the average (or mean) time if necessary.

				Average (mean)

- Plot your results on a line graph on a piece of graph paper. You can stick your graph into your Workbook.

Hint

Remember, a line graph needs both variables to be measured – and here we have numbers for both "Temperature in °C" and "Time for sugar to dissolve in seconds".

c. Analysing and concluding

- Using your graph, what general pattern do you see in your results?

The higher the temperature ______________________________

____

because ______________________________

______________________________.

- Was your prediction correct? Circle your answer.

  Yes **No**

- Explain how you know whether or not your prediction was correct.

____

____

______________________________.

d. Evaluating

- Evaluate your investigation. How can you improve it?
- Explain any improvements suggested.
- Are your results reliable?
- Are there any results that do not follow the pattern?

____

____

____

____

____

Extension

A group decided to investigate how temperature affected the time it takes washing powder to dissolve.

a. Name the variable they will change in each different test.

b. Name the variable they will measure to judge the effect of temperature.

c. Name two variables they need to keep the same.

✓ Checklist

Read each sentence and circle a face for it. Like this:

I understand.

I understand a bit.

I need more help to understand this.

- I can observe, record and begin to explain the changes that take place when some solids are added to water.
- I know that some solids dissolve in water to form solutions and others are insoluble.
- I know that some solids can react with water in irreversible changes.
- I can test which is a pure material and which is a mixture.
- I can investigate factors that affect how quickly materials dissolve.

Glossary

In your own language, write down what these words mean:

dissolve

____

____

evaporate

____

____

filter/filtration

____

____

insoluble

____

____

irreversible

____

____

mix/mixture

____

____

react

____

____

reversible

____

____

separate

____

____

sieve

____

____

solid

____

____

soluble

____

____

solution

____

____

water

____

____

3 Food chains

1 Guess the habitat

Describe a local habitat that you know well.

- What can you tell us about the habitat?

____

____

____

- Where is it?

____

- What is it like to live in this habitat?

____

____

- What types of animals and plants live there?

____

____

Show your description to another group.

Can they guess the place you have described? Circle your answer.

Yes No

Practising my

science language

2 What is the life cycle of a plant?

a. Can you remember a plant's life cycle? Put **A** to **D** in the correct order to show the start of a young plant's life cycle.

A

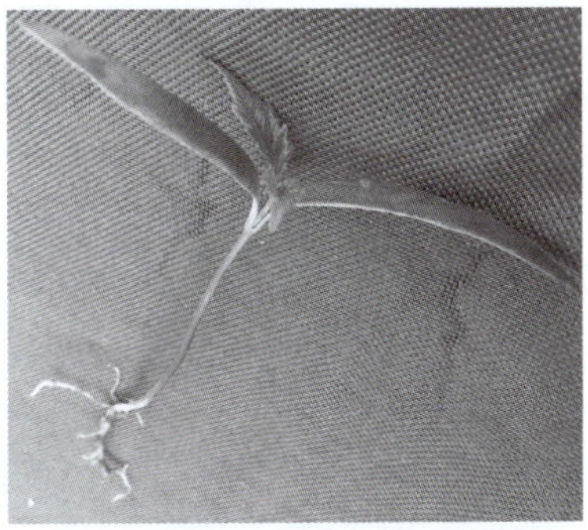

B

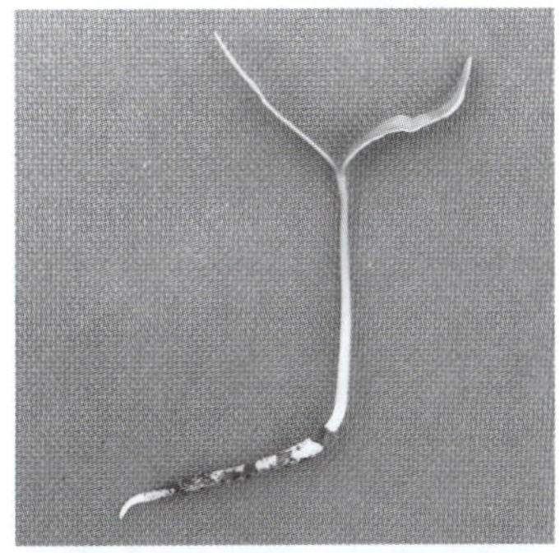

C

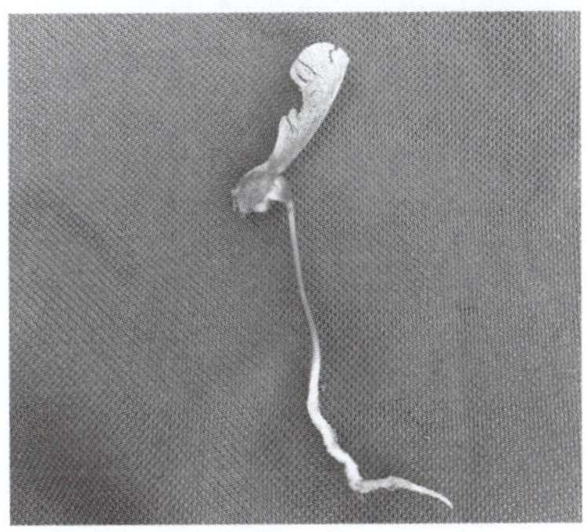

D

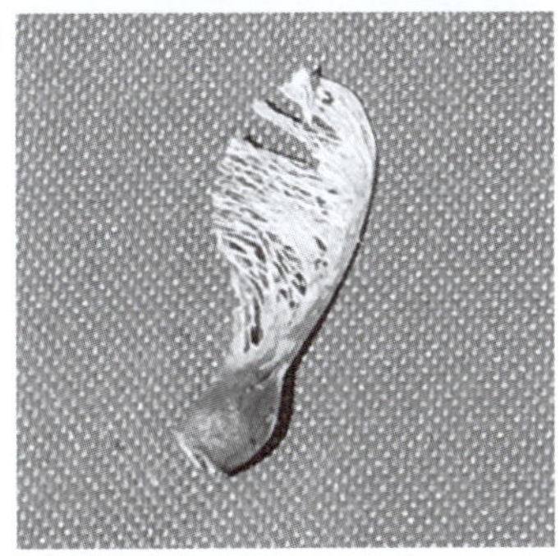

1 ______________________ 2 ______________________

3 ______________________ 4 ______________________

b. What else can you remember? Answer the following questions:

- What do we call the process in which a seed starts to grow? The first letter of the word is given.

  G______________________

- How was the seed dispersed from its parent tree?

  ____

  ____

- Name a habitat where the steps **A** to **D** are most likely to take place in nature.

  ____

3.1 Living things in their habitat

1 Visit a local habitat

Record any plants and animals you observe in a local habitat, using a key if necessary.

Animals	Plants

Extension

Choose one plant and one animal from a local habitat and say how they are well-suited (adapted) to survive in their habitat.

Plant: ____________________

Features that help it survive in its habitat:

____

____

Animal: ____________________

Features that help it survive in its habitat:

____

____

Checklist

Read each sentence and circle a face for it. Like this:

- I understand.
- I understand a bit.
- I need more help to understand this.

- I can use a key to identify living things in a habitat.
- I know how plants and animals depend on each other in their habitats.

3.2 Food chains

Practising my science language

1 Ideas about energy in living things

A group of friends are sharing their ideas about how plants and animals get the energy they need to live.

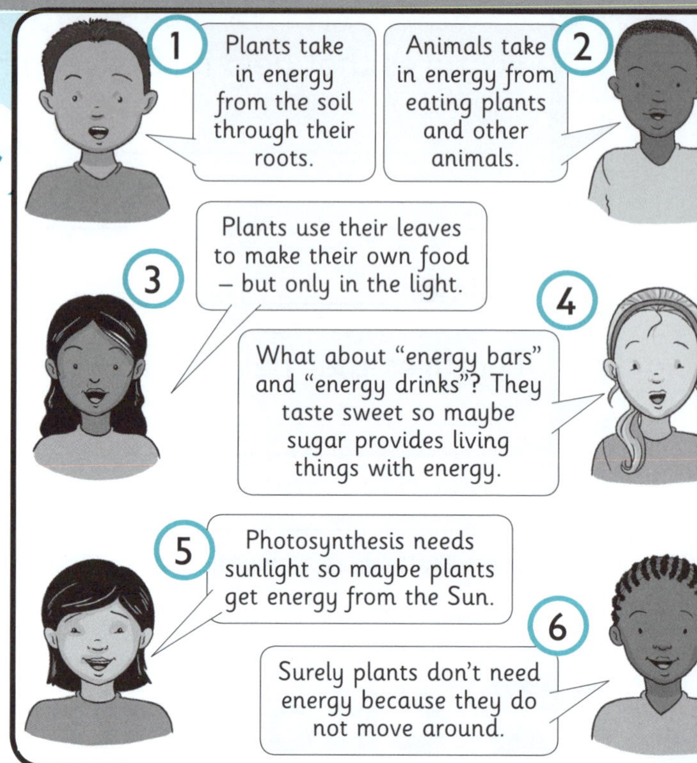

Write what you will say to each person. Tell them if you think their idea (numbered 1 to 6) is good or bad. Circle "good" or "bad" for each idea, then explain why.

Idea 1 – This is a **good** / **bad** idea because ______________________

____.

Idea 2 – This is a **good** / **bad** idea because ______________________

____.

Idea 3 – This is a **good** / **bad** idea because ______________________

____.

Idea 4 – This is a **good** / **bad** idea because ______________________

____.

Idea 5 – This is a **good** / **bad** idea because ______________________

____.

Idea 6 – This is a **good** / **bad** idea because ______________________

____.

2 Constructing your own food chain

a. **Construct** two food chains of your own.

Both food chains must end with a human.

One food chain should be for a vegetarian (a plant-eater). The other food chain should be for a meat-eater.

Draw pictures of each living thing in your food chains.

Food chain ending with a plant-eater:

____

Food chain ending with a meat-eater:

____

b. What difference do you notice about the two food chains?

____

3 Last link in the chain

A large fish that could be the last link is ______________________.

A bird that could be the last link is ______________________.

An aquatic animal that could be the last link is ______________________.

Extension

Consider this food chain:

seaweed → crab → squid → penguin → seal → whale

Imagine that a change to the world's climate results in poor conditions for seaweed growth and after five years all the seaweed has disappeared.

How might this affect the world's penguin population?

____

____

____

____

Checklist

Read each sentence and circle a face for it. Like this:

- I understand.
- I understand a bit.
- I need more help to understand this.

- I know what food chains represent.
- I can show food chains in writing and diagrams.
- I know that food chains always begin with a plant.

3.3 Explaining food chains

1 **What do you remember about germination and plant growth?**

Melissa and Damion are discussing germination and plant growth:

They both have some ideas that are right and some ideas that are wrong.

a. Make a list of Melissa's and Damion's correct ideas about what seeds need to germinate and what plants need to grow.

Melissa's correct ideas	Damion's correct ideas
In germination, seeds need:	In germination, seeds need:
In plant growth, plants need:	In plant growth, plants need:

Practising my science language

2 Producers and consumers

a. With a partner, arrange the following living things into a food chain:

- krill
- bass
- herring
- phytoplankton

Food chain:

________	________	________	________
producer or **consumer**	**producer** or **consumer**	**producer** or **consumer**	**producer** or **consumer**

b. Now circle "producer" or "consumer" below each living thing in your food chain to correctly label each one.

3 Differences between predators and their prey

Look at the photos of the rabbit and the eagle on page 65 of your Student Book.

Record the features (adaptations) of the rabbit and the eagle in the table below.

Useful features of a rabbit	Useful features of an eagle

Extension

a. How do the numbers of living things change from link to link in a food chain?

___

___

b. What might happen to the 2nd and 3rd consumers in a food chain if a disease attacks and kills most of the 1st consumers in a food chain?

___

___

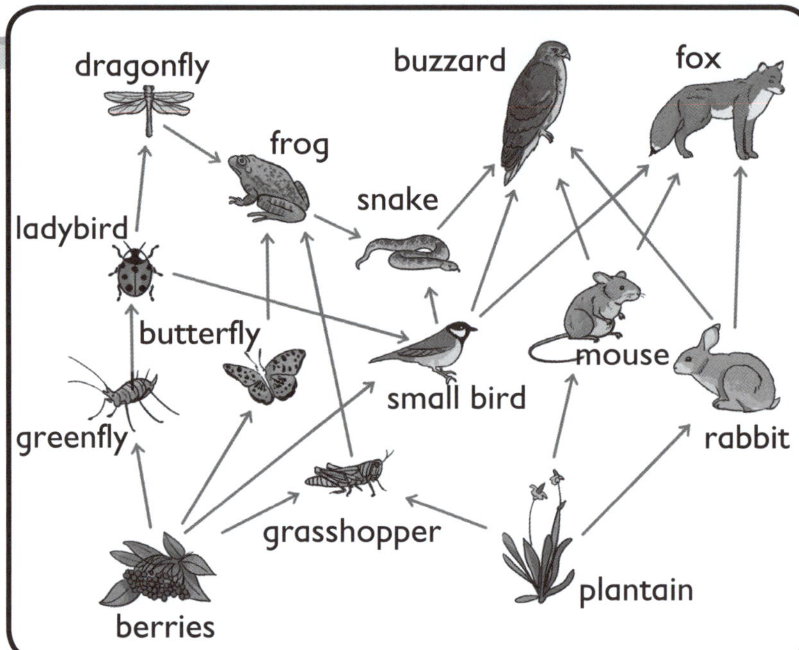

4 Interpreting a food web

a. Answer these questions:

- Name the creatures that rely on berries alone to survive.

  ___

  ___

- Name a predator of the dragonfly.

  ___

- Name the prey of the small birds. ___
- Which predator has the most varied diet? ___
- What do the ladybirds eat? ___
- What do the frogs eat? ___

b. **Draw** two food chains with three links in which the producers are berries.

___

___

Extension

Look back at the food web on page 66 of the Student Book.

a. Write the food chain with the most consumers in this habitat.

____

b. Why can the grasshoppers survive if the plantain are killed by a farmer using weedkiller?

____

____

Checklist

Read each sentence and circle a face for it. Like this:

- I understand.
- I understand a bit.
- I need more help to understand this.

- I can explain why food chains always begin with a plant.
- I can identify and explain in food chains the terms:
  - producer
  - consumer
  - predator
  - prey.
- I can identify the food chains in food webs.

Glossary

In your own language, write down what these words mean:

consumer

____

____

energy

____

____

feeding relationship

____

____

food chain

____

____

food web

____

____

habitat

____

____

plant

____

____

predator

____

____

prey

____

____

producer

____

____

Sun

____

____

4 Electrical conductors and insulators

1 What can you remember about electricity?

a. Draw a mind map linking the words below.

b. Put arrows between any words you link together. Label the arrows, explaining the link between the words.

battery

energy

Electricity

circuit

bulbs

wires

2 Lighting up

a. Use the equipment your teacher supplies to make a circuit to light up the bulb. Draw a labelled diagram of your circuit.

b. Where does the energy in the circuit come from?

____

c. How can you turn the bulb on and off?

____

d. What can you say about the circuit when the bulb is on and when the bulb is off?

Complete each sentence below:

When the bulb is on the circuit is ______________________________.

When the bulb is off the circuit is ______________________________.

4.1 Circuit diagrams

1 Draw your own circuit diagram

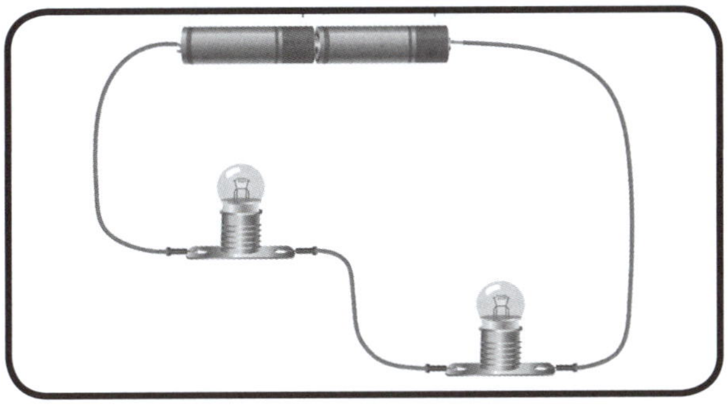

Draw a circuit diagram to represent the circuit shown here.

Practising my science language

2 Alternative circuit diagrams

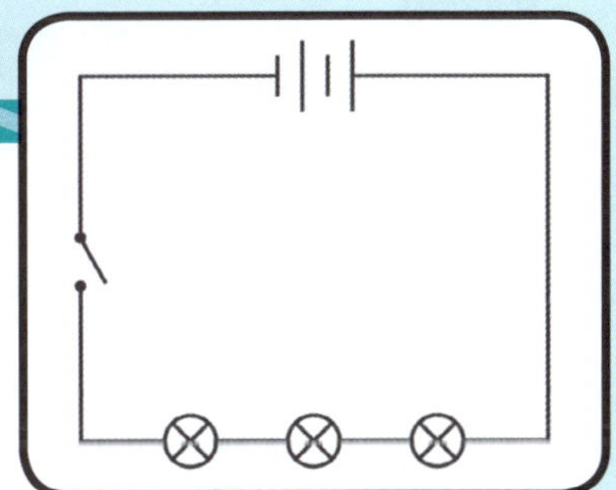

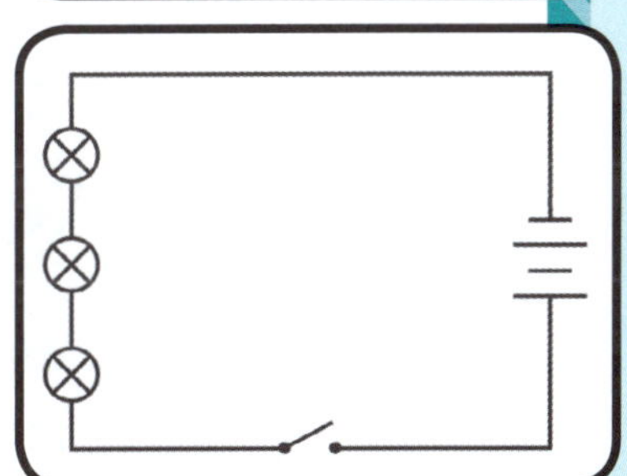

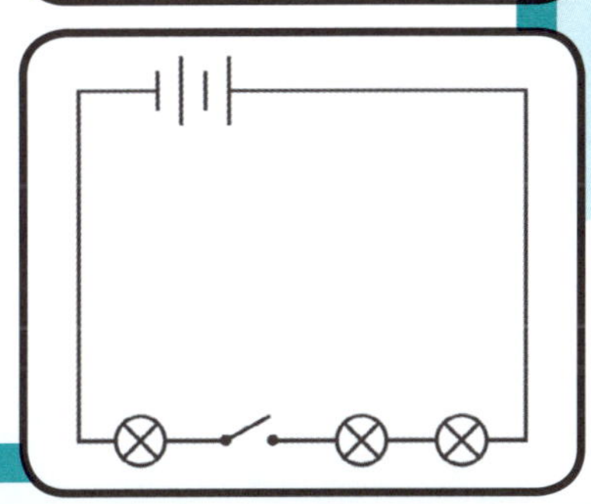

Bastian has designed three different "circuit diagrams". Here are his diagrams:

a. What will you **observe** in each circuit when the switch is closed?

Circle the correct answer in bold below:

I think that **all three bulbs** / **no bulbs** will light up in each circuit.

b. How different are these circuits? What might you say to Bastian?

Circle the correct answer in bold below:

In all three circuits there are **one** / **two** / **three** bulbs in a row when the switch is **open/closed** so the circuits are the **same** / **different**.

Extension

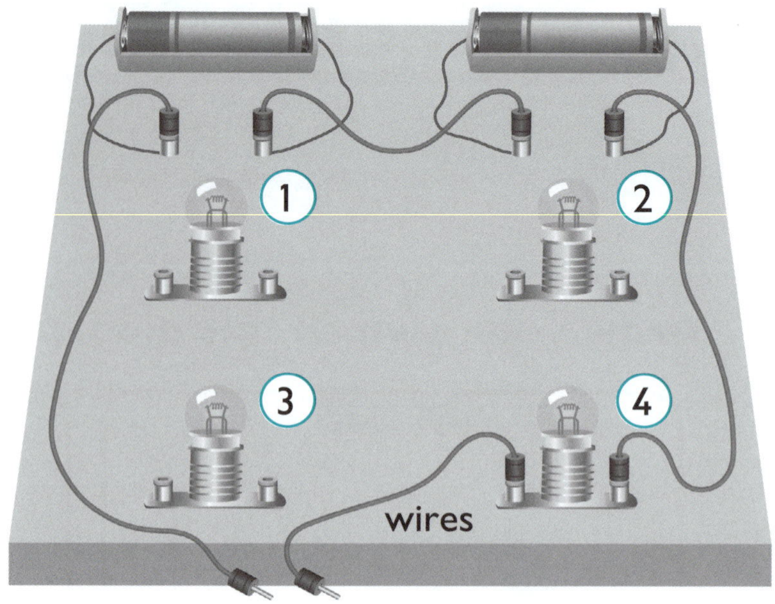

Some schools use **circuit boards** to explore electricity, such as the one shown. Describe how you can move the wires around to:

- make bulbs 1 and 4 light up.

  Connect the wires to ______________________________.

- make only bulb 2 light up.

  Connect the wires to ______________________________.

Checklist

Read each sentence and circle a face for it. Like this:

- I know the symbols of common electrical components.
- I can represent a circuit using a circuit diagram.

4.2 Investigating conductors and insulators

1 Good or poor electrical conductors?

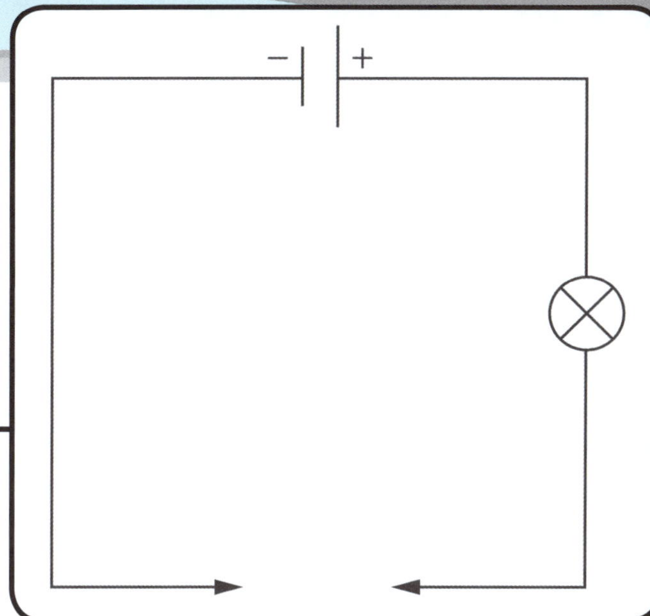

a. Use the circuit alongside to test if electricity can flow through a range of materials.

b. **Record** your results in a table below.

c. Write down the materials the tested objects are made from (not the name of the object itself).

____

____

____

d. What is your **conclusion** from this investigation?

____

2 Checking that graphite conducts electricity

a. Draw the circuit you used to test if graphite conducts electricity.

b. Why would you not test a pencil with a rubber on one end?

4.3 Uses of conductors and insulators

Practising my science language

1 Matching properties and uses

Complete the sentences below using the words in the word box.

conductor	insulators	off	electric shocks	stretched	water

a. Copper is used in the core of the high voltage cable because it is a good ________________ and can be ________________ out to make the thick wires inside the cables.

b. Plastic and rubber are wrapped around the copper core because they are good ________________ and they can protect the copper from ________________.

They also help to prevent ________________, although the electric current is always switched ________________ when electricians work on faulty cables.

2 Your plugs and sockets

Identify which type of plug and socket is used where you live.

Draw a picture of the plug and socket below:

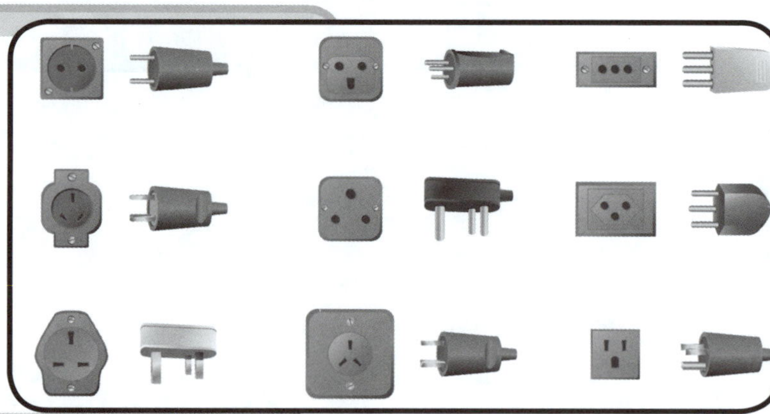

3 Materials in an electric plug

a. Draw a diagram of the inside of a plug.

b. Add the labels “plastic”, “metal” or “metal inside a plastic coating” to show the materials that different parts of the plug are made of.

c. How are different plastics used to prevent us getting an electric shock? Why are they used in the places they are? Circle the correct words in bold below:

The outer casing of the plug is made from a **hard / soft** plastic to protect people who use the plug. The wires inside the plug are coated in **rigid / flexible** plastic so they can be **bent / snapped** easily to make the connections in the plug.

d. Which parts of the plug conduct the electricity? Fill in the missing word below:

All the ________________ parts in a plug can conduct electricity.

Extension

In the space, draw a rough plan of your poster to warn young children starting school about the dangers of electricity.

Checklist

Read each sentence and circle a face for it. Like this:

I understand.

I understand a bit.

I need more help to understand this.

- I can investigate how some materials are better conductors of electricity than others.
- I can classify materials as good conductors of electricity or as electrical insulators.
- I can explain why metals and plastics are used to make plugs and switches.

4.4 Investigating circuits

1 Explaining the model of electric current

Answer the following questions about the "flowing water" model:

a. What does the water pump represent? _______________

b. What part of the water model represents the motor? _____________

c. What do the water pipes represent? _______________

d. How is the electric current represented?

____

e. What can you say about the speed of the flowing water through the water pipes?

____

f. Explain how you could increase the speed of the flowing water and how that relates to a real electric circuit.

____

____

g. Sook has some more questions about the "flowing water" model of an electric current.

Write down what you think after discussing his question with a partner.

____

____

____

____

____

____

2 Testing predictions

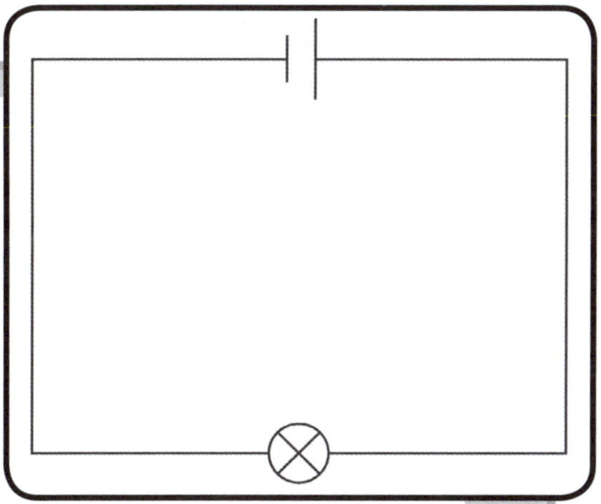

a. With a partner, use the water model to help you predict what will happen in the top circuit when you:

- add another cell (battery) pointing in the same direction as the cell above

  My prediction: ______________________________

  ____

- add another cell pointing in the opposite direction as the cell above

  My prediction: ______________________________

  ____

- add another bulb in the same loop as the first bulb

  My prediction: ______________________________

  ____

- add another bulb in a separate loop as shown.

  My prediction: ______________________________

  ____

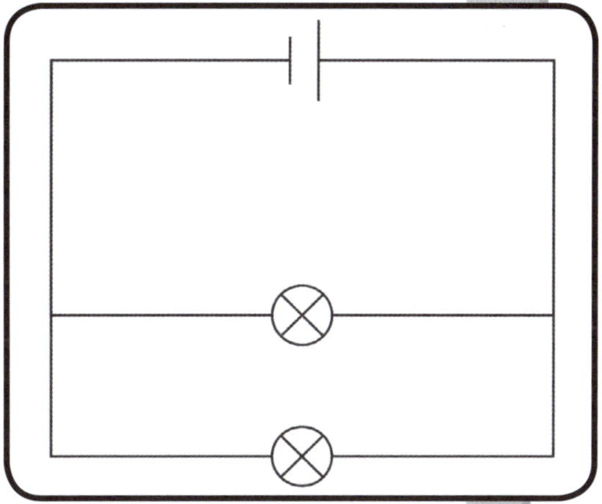

b. Two changes I can make to the first circuit:

1 ______________________________

2 ______________________________

c. Write a question and prediction for each circuit.

Question (circuit 1): ______________________________

____

Prediction: ______________________________

Was your prediction correct? Circle your answer: **Yes** **No**

Question (circuit 2): ______________________________

____

Prediction: ______________________________

Was your prediction correct? Circle your answer: **Yes** **No**

Practising my

science language

3 How does the length of a wire affect how well it conducts electricity?

a. Predicting

- **Predict** the pattern you expect to find. Explain your reasoning.

  The longer the wire, ______________________________.

  This will happen because ______________________________.

b. Planning, carrying out and recording

- What **variable** (or **factor**) are you changing in each test?

  ____

- How will you judge how well the wire is conducting electricity? This will be the variable you will **observe** or measure to judge the effect of changing the length of the wire.

  We will observe the ____________________ of the bulb.

  You can use this circuit as your **plan**:

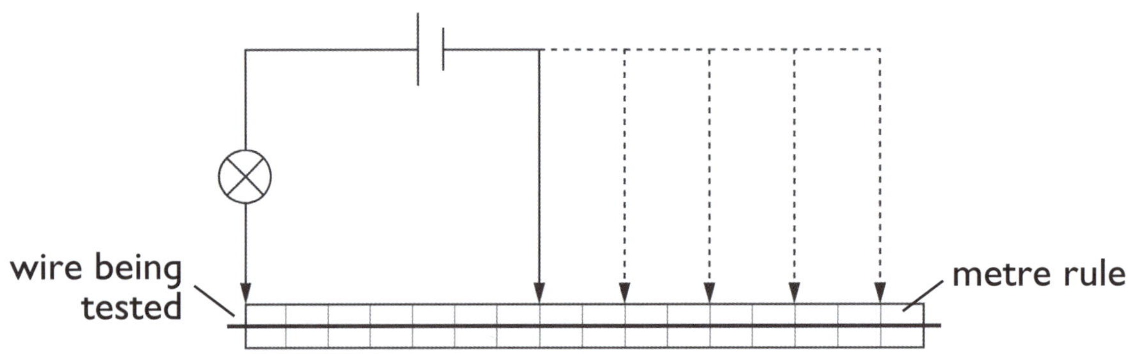

- As you do your **tests** record your observations in the table below:

Length of wire	Brightness of bulb
Short length	
Medium length	
Long length	

c. Analysing and concluding

- When you have finished all your tests, what general pattern do you see in your results?

  The longer the wire, ______________________________.

- Was your prediction correct? Circle your answer: **Yes** **No**

continues on following page ...

... continued from previous page

d. Evaluating

- Evaluate your investigation.
- How can your results be made more reliable?

  Complete the sentence below:

  We can improve the investigation by ________________ the electric current flowing through the wire in each of our tests instead of just judging the ________________ of the bulb.
- Did you **repeat** your tests? Circle your answer: **Yes** **No**
- Were there any results that do not follow the pattern? Circle your answer: **Yes** **No**

Extension

Try to make a bulb light up with a cell, a bulb (no bulb holder) and just one wire. Describe how you managed to make the bulb light up.

____

____

____

Checklist

I understand.

I understand a bit.

I need more help to understand this.

Read each sentence and circle a face for it. Like this:

- I can predict and test the effects of making changes to circuits.
- I can investigate how the length (or thickness) of a wire affects how well it conducts electricity.

Glossary

In your own language, write down what these words mean:

aluminium

battery (cell)

bulb

cable

circuit

circuit board

circuit diagram

conductor

copper

crocodile clips

solid

electric current

electrical

electrical circuit

Glossary

electricity

gold

insulator

iron

lamp

materials

metal

plastic

plug

silver

switch

wire

5 Caring for the environment

1 Animals and environments

Complete the sentences below.

a. The best environment for a worm is ______________________.

b. The best environment for a squirrel is ______________________.

c. The best environment for a cat is ______________________.

2 Can we save the Earth?

In small groups, discuss why the Earth might send out a call for help. How can we protect and help the Earth? Write your thoughts below.

____

____

____

3 Improving your environment

Think about your environment: your home, your school, your village or town.

a. Is it as clean and safe as you would like? Circle your answer. **Yes** **No**

b. List the improvements you would like to see.

____

____

____

____

5.1 Spaceship Earth – the atmosphere

1 What can we do to help the atmosphere?

a. Work with a partner. Discuss what can be done to make the air we breathe cleaner. Make a list of ideas below:

____

____

____

b. Imagine you are in charge of your town or city. What rules can you make to help clean up the air?

____

____

____

____

Extension

How many breaths do you take in a full day?

Count how many breaths you take in a minute. Now complete this calculation:

If we take ______ breaths each minute,

then in one hour we will take

______ × 60 breaths which equals __________.

Therefore, in a whole day we will

take ________________ breaths.

Hint

There are 60 minutes in an hour. There are 24 hours in a day.

Practising my

science language

2 Helping people to understand science

A factory owner and a fisherman live 80 km apart. The fisherman is angry because he has just found out what acid rain is doing to the fish. The factory owner cannot see what the fuss is about.

You know that you can explain what is happening. What will you say to these two people? Can you help both of them?

I will tell them ____

____

____

____

____.

Extension

The gases and smoke from factories can be cleaned and some of the dangerous chemicals removed. This involves a filtration unit placed inside the factory, but it is expensive. Who do you think should pay for it?

I think ______________________________ should pay for it because

____.

3 How important is water?

a. How much water do you drink each day? (One cup is about 300 ml.) Complete the sentences below:

Each day I drink ____________ cups of water.

This means the total volume I drink is about ____________ ml per day.

b. What else do you use water for each day? Make a list of the things you do that require water.

____

____

____

____

4 Why is the atmosphere like a greenhouse?

a. Look at the picture below.

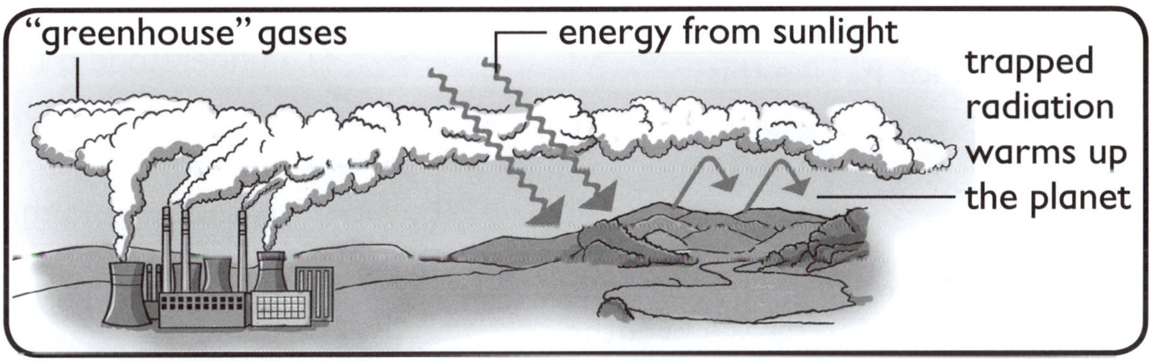

b. With a partner, arrange the five statements so that they tell the story of what happens in the greenhouse effect.

Correct sequence: ____________________

1. The carbon dioxide gas forms a layer of "greenhouse gas" in the Earth's atmosphere.
2. The trapped energy warms up the Earth's surface. This is called global warming.
3. When fossil fuels burn, they produce carbon dioxide.
4. Radiation from the Sun heats up the Earth's surface.
5. The energy radiating from Earth cannot escape through the greenhouse gas layer.

Extension

Write a short paragraph to explain how the three images in the Student Book on page 99 are connected. They show:

- smoke from a factory
- a melting iceberg
- people whose town has been flooded.

____

____

____

____

____

Checklist

Read each sentence and circle a face for it. Like this:

I understand.

I understand a bit.

I need more help to understand this.

- I know the ways in which humans are polluting the air we breathe.
- I can relate a cause to an effect.
- I can explain how pollution from burning fuels causes acid rain.
- I can identify the contribution that human activities make to the greenhouse effect.

5.2 Spaceship Earth – habitats and buildings

Practising my science language

1 Planning for the future: can we agree?

Work in two teams. One team pretends to be gardeners and farmers who enjoy and value green open spaces. The other team are builders and architects who have to find ways of building homes for families. The two teams are soon to meet for a discussion about a new housing development on green parkland.

Here are some phrases that you can use to help prepare for the meeting.

Green spaces are habitats to lots of plants and animals.	Walkers, cyclists and nature lovers all use green spaces.	Fruit, flowers and vegetables need space to grow.	Green plants make oxygen for us to breathe.
People cannot live on grassland. People need shelter from rain, wind and sun.	There are more people in the world. They need more homes.	Is there a solution that helps everyone?	Homes can also contain plants. Families can keep animals as pets.

a. Spend five minutes planning what you will say to each other.

Circle your role. **gardener** **farmer** **builder** **architect**

- What arguments will you make to the other team?

____

____

____

- What arguments do you think the other team will make?

____

____

- Can you reach a compromise? **Yes** **No**

continues on following page …

... continued from previous page

b. Meet the other team. Listen to each other and share your ideas. Always listen carefully and be polite.

- What agreements have you made?

____

____

____

- What was the decision?

____

____

____

- What **conclusions** did you come to together?

____

____

____

Extension

Why does loss of biodiversity matter?

____

____

____

Practising my science language

2 Case study

a. Use the internet to research forest areas that need **protecting**. For example, you can explore what is happening to preserve the Satpuda Maikal forest and all of its animals and plants.

The forest that I have researched is ______________________________.

continues on following page ...

… continued from previous page

b. The World Wide Fund for Nature (WWF) is the world's leading independent conservation organisation. Look at the WWF's website on the internet. Find out three things about its work in Satpuda Maikal and other forest areas that are under threat.

1 ______________________________

____

2 ______________________________

____

3 ______________________________

____

Checklist

I understand.

I understand a bit.

I need more help to understand this.

Read each sentence and circle a face for it. Like this:

- I know how important green spaces are for healthy living.
- I know about deforestation and how it is harming important habitats and species.
- I have researched how humans ensure that habitats and species are protected.

5.3 Spaceship Earth – save energy and recycle

1 Can you imagine a world without fuel?

Imagine a world in the future where there is no more coal, no more oil and no more natural gas. With a partner, make a list of the problems that you might face if you lived in the world at that time.

Hint

- What will the world be like to live in?
- How will your life be changed?
- What problems might you face?

Without fossil fuels:

____

____

____

____

____

____

____

____

____

____

____

____

____

____

2 Let us think about our own waste

Your teacher will provide your group with a bag of waste items.

Hint

Your bag of waste materials might contain glass and sharp metal – take care.

a. Spread the waste on the table and **identify** each item. List them here.

____

____

____

b. Sort the waste items into groups of different materials.

c. Use a balance to weigh the total amount of card/paper, the total amount of plastics, the total amount of glass, and the total amount of metal.

Card/paper: ______________

Plastics: ______________

Glass: ______________

Metal: ______________

d. Draw a bar chart to show the different amounts of waste in the bag.

3 Waste from towns and cities

a. Working in a group, research what happens to the waste from your home, village, town or city.

- Find out where all of the waste trucks go.
- Does any waste get recycled, buried or burned? What happens to it?
- Find out where there is a landfill site near where you live.

Make some notes below:

b. Design a poster that informs people about what happens to their waste. The poster should tell readers about types of waste, about recycling and about disposing of waste.

You can sketch some ideas here, but should produce your final poster on a separate, large piece of paper.

4 Making connections

Consider the set of story cards below.

Arrange the cards in the correct order so that they tell a story from Card 1 to Card 7:

Card 1 You forget to turn off the light.

Card 2 ____________________

Card 3 ____________________

Card 4 ____________________

Card 5 ____________________

Card 6 ____________________

Card 7 Floods make people homeless.

Practising my

science language

5 Explaining the problem to others

Work with a partner to design an information leaflet about one particular environmental problem. You may want to do some research of your own to find out more. Make sure that you include some advice to people about what they can do to help solve the problem.

The problem our leaflet will address is ______________________________.

Use the space below to sketch out your ideas.

Create your leaflet on a single sheet of paper that can be folded twice to make a "trifold" leaflet.

Extension

Sometimes it might seem impossible for a single person to help solve a problem that is worldwide. Do you think an individual can have an effect on the whole planet? In what ways?

____

____

____

____

Checklist

Read each sentence and circle a face for it. Like this:

- I understand.
- I understand a bit.
- I need more help to understand this.

- I understand the importance of saving fossil fuels for the future.
- I know that recycling waste can save energy and reduce landfill.
- I can identify the ways that waste can be recycled.
- I can communicate ideas about environmental problems and solutions.

5.4 Spaceship Earth – taking care of my local environment

1 Care for your school

a. In what ways do you look after and care for your school environment? Work with your partner to identify the things that you do or that others do in your school.

____

____

____

b. Is your school a "green" school? Why or why not?

____

____

2 Litter study

In this study you will do an investigative search around your school.

What did your group find out about:

- the number of litter bins inside school?

  ____

- the number of litter bins outside school?

  ____

- the need for better or more litter bins?

  ____

- litter in your school?

  ____

3 Energy study

In a small group, carry out an energy study of your school. A full energy study might take you at least an hour to complete.

a. Are there lights turned on that are not needed? Are the lights using low energy LED bulbs? How many? All of them? Half of them?

____

____

____

____

b. Are the hot water taps turned off or are they dripping and wasting energy?

____

____

c. Are some rooms too hot and some too cold? Use a thermometer to find the temperature in four rooms.

Room 1: ________________ °C

Room 2: ________________ °C

Room 3: ________________ °C

Room 4: ________________ °C

- Which temperature is best for learning?

  ________________ °C

- Does your school waste energy through windows and doors?

  Yes **No**

d. How can your school save energy?

Our school can save energy by ______________________________

____

____

____

____.

4 Waste recycling study

Does your school already recycle any waste products (aluminium cans, plastic bottles, paper, and so on)? If it does, complete part **a.**; if not, complete part **b**.

a. Work in your group to find out the following and then write a report about recycling at your school.

- How much waste is recycled each week or over a one-month period?

  ____

- Who collects the waste to be recycled?

  ____

- What happens to the recycled waste?

  ____

b. Work as a class to start a "recycling centre" in your classroom. Plan this with your teacher and others in your class.

Hint

Perhaps your teacher can invite the people who collect the waste to be recycled into the classroom to say a few words to your class about the job of recycling.

- How will you collect items?

  ____

  ____

- Which items are easiest to collect and recycle?

  ____

- How will you label the containers?

  ____

  ____

- Who will be in charge of emptying the containers when they are full?

  ____

  ____

5 Identifying habitats

a. As a class, take a habitat walk around your school building. Take a photograph or draw two areas that you think are habitats for particular animals.

Habitat 1	Habitat 2

b. What sorts of animals live in these two habitats in and around your school? Write a list below:

6 Protecting and improving habitats

a. Work with a partner to design or make an improvement for one of the habitats in your school grounds. For example, are there enough feeding areas and sleeping areas? Perhaps you can design and make some extra shelters for particular creatures.

Make some notes below:

One habitat we can improve is ____________________.

The habitat can be improved by ____________________.

The animals that live in this habitat are ____________________.

b. Take a photograph or draw a sketch below to include in your design.

Extension

a. In a small group, draw a mind map on A4 paper to **suggest** improvements that might make the habitats around your home even better for the wildlife. You can use some of the words and phrases in the word box to help you get started.

bat box   pick up litter   leave an area in the garden to grow wild
compost waste   bird box   planting bee-friendly flowers
create a wildlife area   leave gap in fence for hedgehogs
avoid using pesticides

b. Your teacher can then use your mind maps to create a class display.

Checklist

Read each sentence and circle a face for it. Like this:

I understand.

I understand a bit.

I need more help to understand this.

- I have investigated ways that my school can use less energy.
- I have observed and recorded how litter is managed in my school.
- I can describe how a habitat can be protected and improved.

Glossary

In your own language, write down what these words mean:

acid rain

greenhouse effect

deforestation

habitat

effects

landfill

energy consumption

litter

environment

negative effect/impact

fossil fuel

pollution

Glossary

positive

protect/protection

raw materials

recycle/recycling

reduce

species

waste

6 Mass and weight

1 Poetry in motion

Write your own four-line poem about forces.

____

____

____

____

2 Finding forces

a. Look at the picture below:

b. Circle any forces you can find. One has been done for you.

6.1 Investigating mass and weight

Extension

Carry out some research to find out about other problems that Isaac Newton worked on. Make some notes below.

____

____

____

____

____

Practising my science language

1 Use a forcemeter

a. With a partner, use a forcemeter to measure the weight of some everyday objects shown on page 119 of the Student Book.

b. Record your measurements in the table below.

Object	Weight in newtons (N)
pencil case	
shoe	
1 kg mass	

2 Food labels

a. At home, find some packets, jars, tins or boxes of food that have a mass label.

b. Complete the table below using your own examples. One has been done for you.

Object	Mass in grams or kilograms (g or kg)	Weight in newtons (N)
jar of jam	340 g = 0.34 kg	3.4 N

3 Mass and weight

On Earth, every 1 kg mass feels a downward pull of gravity of about 10 N. That is how strong the Earth's gravity is.

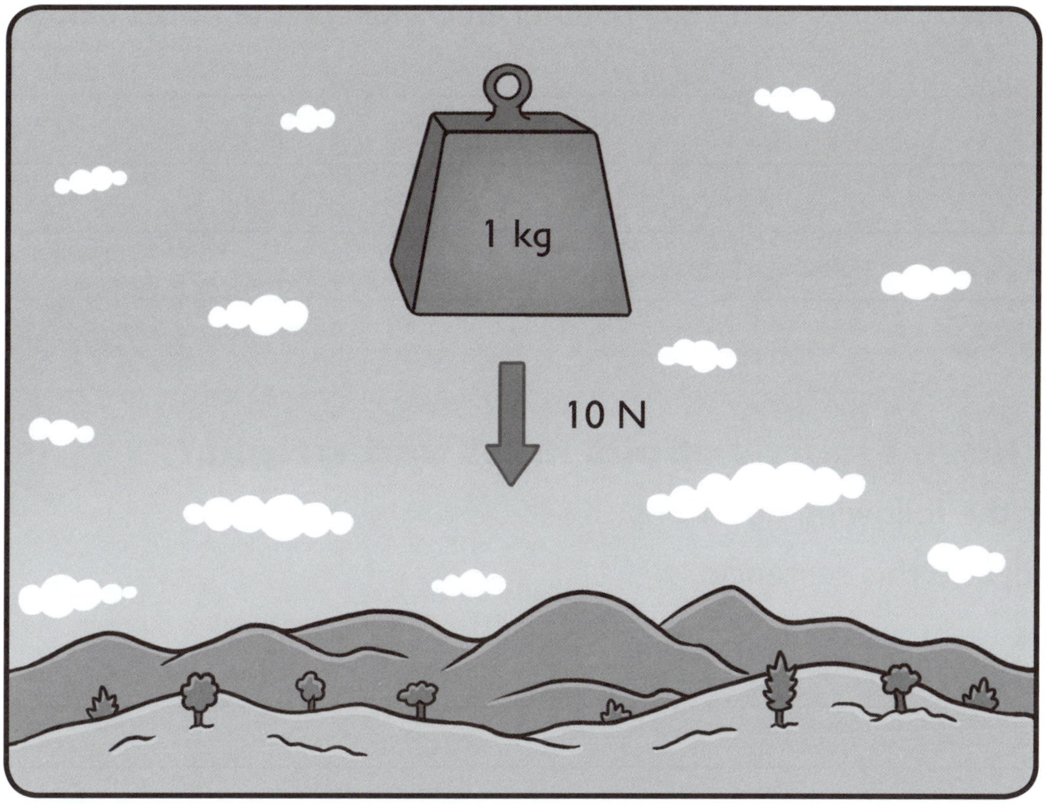

With a partner, discuss and then complete the mass and weight table below. The first row has been done for you.

Object	Mass in grams or kilograms (g or kg)	Weight in newtons (N)
Bag of potatoes	2 kg	20
Adult	74 kg	
Jar of pickles	500 g = 0.5 kg	
Pencil	100 g = ____________ kg	
Fido the dog		250

4 Explaining mass and weight

How can you explain the difference between mass and weight to someone who has been absent from today's class?

Share your thoughts with your partner and make some notes below.

____

____

____

____

5 What have I learnt about mass and weight?

Answer the following questions.

a. Complete this sentence:

Mass is the amount of stuff in something but weight is

____

______________________________.

b. Estimate how many newtons a cat with a mass of 4 kg would weigh.

____

c. All planets have gravity. What do you know about gravity on Earth?

____

____

____

d. Cosmonaut Yuri decided to take a 2 kg box of sugar cubes to the Moon.

How will the box of sugar cubes compare to when it was on Earth? Tick the four correct answers below:

- ☐ It will have the same mass.
- ☐ It will have the same taste.
- ☐ It will have the same weight.
- ☐ It will have the same shape.
- ☐ It will have the same number of cubes.

Extension

The mass of this book is 1.5 kg.

a. What will the mass of the book be when taken to the Moon?

The mass of the book will be

________________ kg.

b. How will its weight (in newtons) change?

____

c. Explain your answers to the questions above.

____

____

Checklist

Read each sentence and circle a face for it. Like this:

- I understand.
- I understand a bit.
- I need more help to understand this.

- I can explain the difference between the mass and the weight of an object.
- I can use a forcemeter to measure weight.
- I can use the unit of force (including weight) and the units of mass.
- I can calculate the weight of an object when I know its mass.

6.2 Forces and force diagrams

Practising my **science language**

1 Describing forces

Here are Kasem and Jini applying some types of force. Work with a partner to describe the different forces in each picture.

Picture A ______________________________

____

Picture B ______________________________

____

Picture C ______________________________

____

Picture D ______________________________

____

2 Using force arrows

a. Look at the diagram. Akim says he cannot see any forces in this diagram. "The cup is not moving," he says. Myra disagrees and wants to add her arrows to show the forces.

b. What do you think? Can you see the forces at work?

c. Cut out a paper arrow and use it to show where there are forces on the diagram. With several arrows, you can show all of the forces in the diagram.

3 Exploring the effects of forces

You will be given a tennis ball or squash ball to investigate the effects of different forces.

Work with a partner. Discuss and make notes about how you can apply forces to make the ball:

a. change size or shape ______________________________

____

b. speed up ______________________________

____

c. slow down ______________________________

____

d. change direction ______________________________

____

Extension

a. Match the force described in each picture (A to D in Question 1 on page 96) to its effect listed below. Draw lines to link the picture to their effects. Think carefully, as there may be more than one effect. One has been done for you.

	Effect
Picture A	1 Forces can change the size or shape of an object.
Picture B	2 Forces can make an object speed up or slow down.
Picture C	3 Forces can make a moving object change its direction.
Picture D	

b. Discuss with a partner the direction of the force(s) being applied in pictures A to D. Then position your paper arrows on the page in the right place and ask your teacher to check.

Extension

a. Imagine a hard ball with three equal pushing forces acting on it. The ball is stationary – it is not moving.

Draw a ball and the position of the three forces.

b. One of the three forces is suddenly removed. What will happen to the ball?

Draw a picture to help you explain. Use blue force arrows and a red arrow to show any movement of the ball.

Checklist

Read each sentence and circle a face for it. Like this:

- I understand.
- I understand a bit.
- I need more help to understand this.

- I can name different types of force.
- I can use arrows to show the direction of a force.
- I can recognise the effects a force can have on an object.
- I can explain what happens when forces are balanced and when they are unbalanced.

6.3 Friction

1 Friction on the table

Choose a book and give it a short, sharp push across the table. Do not push the book hard enough to fall off the table!

a. With a partner, discuss why the book stops moving.

The book stops moving because ________________________________

____.

b. Draw a diagram that has a force arrow to show what is happening when the book speeds up as you apply a force.

continues on following page …

… continued from previous page

c. Draw a diagram that has a force arrow to show what is happening when the book slows down.

2 Examples of friction in action

a. List three examples of where friction is useful to us.

Example 1: ______________________________

____

Example 2: ______________________________

____

Example 3: ______________________________

____

b. Write down three examples of where friction is not helpful to us.

Example 1: ______________________________

____

Example 2: ______________________________

____

Example 3: ______________________________

____

3 Car design

Cars have to force their way through the air on every journey they make.

a. Design a streamlined car that will reduce the force of air resistance.

Streamlined car:

b. Draw a car that will experience high air resistance forces.

Car with high air resistance forces:

c. Give two advantages of the streamlined car over your other design.

Advantage 1: ______________________________

____

Advantage 2: ______________________________

____

4 Make and check a prediction

a. Work with a partner and collect two pieces of A4 paper.

Crumple up one sheet to test and compare against the other flat sheet.

b. **Predict** which piece of paper will feel the least air resistance when it is dropped: the crumpled-up sheet of paper or the flat sheet of paper.
Tick your answer below:

☐ A crumpled-up sheet of paper will feel the least air resistance

☐ A flat sheet of paper will feel the least air resistance

- Explain your prediction. ______________________________

____

- Now check your prediction. Was it correct?
  Cirle your answer. **Yes** **No**
- How did you make this a fair test between the two pieces of paper?

____

____

- Draw a diagram that helps to explain the results of your test.

c. Using the flat sheet of paper:

- Fold and make a shape that should fall faster than the crumpled-up sheet of paper.
- Test your design against the crumpled piece of paper.
- What happened?

____

____

5 Making a model parachute

Draw a labelled diagram of your model parachute and skydiver.

Practising my

science language

6 Investigating parachutes

a. In small groups, decide which factor (variable) you want to investigate.

We will investigate ______________________________

______________________________.

Therefore, the question to investigate is:

How does ______________________ affect the time it takes the parachute to fall to the ground?

b. Make and explain your prediction.

I think that ______________________________

because ______________________________

______________________________.

continues on following page ...

... continued from previous page

c. Plan a fair test. Include a list of equipment (apparatus) that you will need to carry out your plan.

____

____

____

____

____

____

d. Explain why it is a good idea to repeat each test.

It is a good idea to repeat each test because ______________________________

____

______________________________.

e. Record all the data you have collected in a table in the space below.

continues on following page ...

... continued from previous page

f. Display your results on a graph. Decide whether to use a **bar chart** or a **line graph**.

Tick your answer:

☐ Bar chart

☐ Line graph

g. Draw your **conclusions** from the evidence gathered in your investigation. Explain your findings.

h. **Evaluate** your investigation. Justify any changes you would make.

Extension

Place a 1 kg mass inside an empty margarine or ice-cream tub.

You will be given two sheets of sandpaper. One is very rough (made by sticking large grains of sand to the paper). The other is smoother (because it is made with small, fine grains of sand).

a. Predict which sandpaper will grip the base of the tub better. Tick your answer:

☐ Rough sandpaper

☐ Smooth sandpaper

b. Was the result surprising? Circle your answer. **Yes** **No**

c. Try to explain your result.

____

____

____

Checklist

I understand.

I understand a bit.

I need more help to understand this.

Read each sentence and circle a face for it. Like this:

- I can explain the force of friction.
- I know that air resistance is a type of friction.
- I can investigate how friction affects the movement of objects.

Glossary

In your own language, write down what these words mean:

air resistance

____

____

balanced

____

____

direction

____

____

energy

____

____

force

____

____

forcemeter

____

____

friction

____

____

gram (g)

____

____

gravity

____

____

kilogram (kg)

____

____

mass

____

____

matter

____

____

Glossary

move/moving

speed up

newtons (N)

unbalanced

slow down

weight